Higher

English

2000 Exam
Interpretation
Analysis and Appreciation

2001 Exam
Close Reading
Analysis and Appreciation

2002 Exam
Close Reading
Analysis and Appreciation

Specimen Question Paper
(for exams in and after 2003)
Close Reading
Critical Essay

2003 Exam
Close Reading
Critical Essay

© Scottish Qualifications Authority

All rights reserved. Copying prohibited. No part of this publication may be reproduced, stored in a retrieval system, or transmitted in any form or by any means, electronic, mechanical, photocopying, recording or otherwise.

First exam published in 2000.
Published by
Leckie & Leckie, 8 Whitehill Terrace, St. Andrews, Scotland KY16 8RN
tel: 01334 475656 fax: 01334 477392
enquiries@leckieandleckie.co.uk www.leckieandleckie.co.uk

Leckie & Leckie Project Team: Peter Dennis; John MacPherson; Bruce Ryan; Andrea Smith

ISBN 1-84372-121-X

A CIP Catalogue record for this book is available from the British Library.

Printed in Scotland by Scotprint.

Leckie & Leckie is a division of Granada Learning Limited, part of Granada plc.

Scotland's leading educational publishers

Introduction

Dear Student,

This past paper book provides you with the perfect opportunity to put into practice everything you should know in order to excel in your exams. The compilation of papers will expose you to an extensive range of questions and will provide you with a clear idea of what to expect in your own exam this summer.

The past papers represent an integral part of your revision: the questions test not only your subject knowledge and understanding but also the examinable skills that you should have acquired and developed throughout your course. The answer booklet at the back of the book will allow you to monitor your ability, see exactly what an examiner looks for to award full marks and will also enable you to identify areas for more concentrated revision. Make use too of the tips for revision and sitting your exam to ensure you perform to the best of your ability on the day.

Practice makes perfect. This book should prove an invaluable revision aid and will help you prepare to succeed.

Good luck!

Acknowledgements

Leckie & Leckie is grateful to the copyright holders, as credited, for permission to use their material. Every effort has been made to trace the copyright holders and to obtain their permission for the use of copyright material. Leckie & Leckie will gladly receive information enabling them to rectify any error or omission in subsequent editions.

'Originally' is taken from *The Other Country* by Carol Ann Duffy published by Anvil Press Poetry in 1990 (2001 Analysis and Appreciation p 2);
Extract from *Big Bangs* by Howard Goodall published by Chatto & Windus. Used by permission of The Random House Group Limited (2002 Close Reading p 2);
The article 'Warming Up For The Ice Age' by Angus Clark © The Times Newspapers Ltd (2000) (2003 SQP Close Reading p 2);
The article 'Stormy Weather' by James O. Jackson © Time Magazine (2003 SQP Close Reading p 2);
The article 'Can Britain Afford to Keep Talented Immigrants Out?' by Ruth Wishart © The Herald June 2002 (2003 Close Reading p 2);
Palgrave Macmillan for an extract from *Lost in Music* by Giles Smith (2002 Close Reading p 3);
The article 'We Have Been Here Before' by Anne Karpf © Guardian Newspapers Ltd June 2002 (2003 Close Reading p 3).

The following companies/individuals have very generously given permission to reproduce their copyright material free of charge:

Extract from *I'm a Little Special – a Muhammed Ali Reader* by Gerald Early published by Yellow Jersey Press. Used by permission of the Random House Group Limited (2001 Close Reading p 3);
Guardian Newspapers Ltd for an extract of an article by Neil Ascherson (2000 Interpretation p 2).

20000 HIGHER

X039/301

NATIONAL
QUALIFICATIONS
2000

WEDNESDAY, 24 MAY
9.00 AM – 10.30 AM

ENGLISH AND COMMUNICATION
HIGHER
Interpretation

You should attempt all questions.

The total value of the Paper is 60 marks.

PIB X039/301 6/3/9520

SCOTTISH
QUALIFICATIONS
AUTHORITY

There are TWO passages and questions.

Read both passages carefully and then answer all the questions which follow. **Use your own words whenever possible and particularly when you are instructed to do so.**

You should read each passage to:

understand what each writer is saying about old age and society's attitudes towards old people (**Understanding—U**);

analyse each writer's choice of language, imagery and structures to recognise how they convey the point of view and contribute to the impact of the passage (**Analysis—A**);

evaluate how effectively each writer has achieved the purpose (**Evaluation—E**).

A code letter (U, A, E) is used alongside each question to give some indication of the skills being assessed. The number of marks attached to each question will give some indication of the length of answer required.

PASSAGE 1

In the first passage, Neil Ascherson, a distinguished journalist with "The Observer" newspaper, considers society's attitude towards old age and old people.

Last November 11th, old men and old women were doing what they are supposed to do best—remembering. They were 100 years old, more or less, as they stood or sat by the Cenotaph in
5 London and the Menin Gate at Ypres. They said: "Don't ever forget" and they were thinking of the millions who died young in the Great War. But it will be difficult to forget them either. They were few, but standing for the millions who are not dead
10 but simply old.

In a generation, living to 100 will be common. As the medical revolution of the twenty-first century replaces drugs with human spare parts grown from cell tissue, fit and mentally lively men and women
15 in their nineties will be common. Society is still utterly unprepared for this change. Chatter about "grey power", or even the growing and admirable concern for the old and helpless who are not cared for by families, have scarcely touched the problem.
20 The old, still veiled in outworn stereotypes and new-fangled prejudice, are the Great Excluded.

It is time to rewrite the Seven Ages of Man. When Shakespeare wrote about them, living beyond 60 was a rarity. Life was too short for what was
25 expected of human beings—not too long.

Now, though, the demographic tide is flowing in the opposite direction. In 1961, 6·2 million people in the United Kingdom were aged 65 or over. Today, it is nearly nine million; in 2021 it is
30 projected to be 11·7 million. The real leap here is at the top of the range: the proportion of those over 80. This group, which formed less than 2% in 1961, numbers about 4% now, but will reach 5% by 2021, when Britain will have about 30,000
35 centenarians. Life expectancy at birth was 58·4 years for men in 1931, and 62·4 years for women. Today, it is about 74 for men and almost 80 for women.

The figures don't add up to an unmixed disaster scenario. Unless the economy collapses, British 40 governments during the next generation can perfectly well afford to go on paying the present levels of state old-age pension, and could almost certainly afford to raise it in terms of real income. The problem here is political will rather than 45 financial capacity. The pinch will come in other resource areas, such as health spending. People over 65 consume three times as many prescription items as other age groups. Nearly half those with some measure of disability are over 70. 50

But the resource question, meeting the material needs of the old and elderly, is only half the story. The real problem lies elsewhere—in the imagination. What are the old for? Who are they, and do the traditional divisions of human life into 55 childhood, youth, middle age and old age still fit our experience?

You are not necessarily as old as you feel, but you are as old as other people feel you are. Age is a construct, a pattern woven by our society which 60 changes out of recognition as times change. For us, as for Shakespeare, male old age must imply the loss of physical beauty, the coming of "shrunk shanks", loose paunches and the rest.

In contrast, classical taste produced statuary 65 which showed old men with huge muscled shoulders, as if a life of physical labour left bodies more powerful than ever. Nothing remains of this view now; the idea of old men as images of strength rather than objects for "compassion" has become 70 repellent. When 1960s astronaut Senator John Glenn returned to space at the age of 77, he was celebrated as an exception to the rule. But when something happens which seems to challenge the general condescension towards the old, there is a 75 roar of virtuous disapproval from younger generations.

Even the universal image of old age as the time of superior wisdom is passing away. We no longer
80 have Elders whose counsel is precious and who must be respected. This debunking was already underway with Shakespeare's sardonic Seven Ages in *As You Like It*. For him, life after about 40 was already crumbling into absurdity. In our own
85 times, grandmothers are still expected to remember—that much of their function remains—but their habit of giving advice, and requiring attention to be paid to their advice, is no longer wanted. The old have been excommunicated and they resent it. 90

47% of people over 75 live alone and frequently revert to their existence as teenagers. Their room is a tip of familiar possessions; they eat any old biscuits or cold sausages lying around; they delight in doing things their way; they have their own 95 special circle of friends; they are usually deaf, but specially deaf to the scoldings of the authoritarian young. One day, society will realise this and invent a new purpose for the old. Until then, they must find their own reasons to survive. 100

PASSAGE 2

The second passage is taken from a collection of writing by mature women entitled "New Ideas for Getting the Most Out of Life". Here, Mary Cooper explains how and why she intends to continue to grow old "disgracefully".

How am I growing old disgracefully? Well, you wouldn't be shocked by my appearance if you met me in the street. And I wouldn't be likely to embarrass you if we stood talking.

5 For me growing old disgracefully is more an attitude to old age, a defying of its stereotypes, than an outrageous way of behaving. It is a necessary countering of the negative words and images associated with women's ageing: "old hag", "old
10 bag", "old biddy" and so on.

It is OK for me now, for instance, to be an old woman on my own. It's true the world we know best is organised around couples, usually husband and wife, but there is a good life to be had as an old
15 woman who is not part of a couple but who is part of a social network which includes a whole range of relationships.

When we are old there is more time for gossiping (men talk and discuss; women gossip, don't they?).
20 I see old women together arm in arm negotiating a slippery pavement or rough steps. I see them with their trolleys gossiping together in the supermarket and I rejoice that we have each other, that the older we grow the more women of our own
25 age there are around us. We are not going to be identified as "a growing social problem", as the social commentators would have us labelled, but as a thriving, gossiping and defiant sisterhood.

Yes, there is the fumbling, the constant mislaying of
30 belongings, the forgetting of the right words and names but that happened when I was young too! Now I've got four competent daughters who enjoy putting me right. Now and again I want to remind them where I've been and what I've done with my life . . . "Never apologise! Never make excuses," I 35 say to myself when this happens. "It only draws attention to the lapse. Move on to the next thing! If *they* still need to prove themselves, I don't." So I relax and resolve to remember the word—or whatever—next time and to have a laugh with my 40 friends about it when we next meet.

Most of all, growing old disgracefully for me means that both the free, happy, playful child *and* the wise old woman are kept alive inside, both together, in my heart and in my head. This can't 45 just happen; there have to be opportunities made and taken—joining in the silly games, or better still starting one off! And the wise old woman? I think the modern word for wisdom is self-awareness. And self-awareness, a critical self-awareness, is 50 best kept alive by listening, by listening and learning—that will do for a start anyway.

Before I was a feminist, growing old disgracefully might have meant something quite different— being shameful, even wicked—at the very least, 55 doing things my mother would have disapproved of! Now it means being more myself than I've ever been before! And that feels pretty good—most of the time!

I remember an occasion many years ago when my 60 sister and I were watching an old fairground organ playing a waltz. We longed to dance together with the music but we were surrounded by our children. Their presence weighed us down. Then suddenly we both stepped into the open space in front of the 65 organ, dancing together. It was a moment none of us has ever forgotten! So daring! So disgraceful! I cherish the memory; it holds the feeling I want to carry with me through my old age.

Questions on Passage 1

Marks *Code*

1. "Don't ever forget" (line 6)

   By referring to paragraph one, identify the two groups of people whom we should not forget.

   2 U

2. "In a generation, living to 100 will be common." (line 11)

   (*a*) Explain fully the reason the writer gives for this statement. (Use your own words as far as possible in your answer.)

   2 U

   (*b*) By referring to lines 15–21 ("Society is . . . Great Excluded."), explain fully the difficulties that such longevity causes.

   2 U

3. "Now, though, the demographic tide is flowing in the opposite direction." (lines 26–27)

   (*a*) Analyse the image used by the writer in this sentence.

   2 U/A

   (*b*) Show how effective you find the image in the context of lines 22–38.

   2 E

4. "The figures don't add up to an unmixed disaster scenario." (lines 39–40)

   Explain the meaning of the sentence. Go on to explain how the ideas of the sentence are developed in the rest of the paragraph.

   4 U

5. (*a*) In lines 51–57, identify **two** features of sentence structure which mark a shift in the writer's line of thought.

   2 A

   (*b*) In your own words, explain this new line of thought. You should refer to lines 53–61 ("The real problem . . . as times change.") in your answer.

   2 U

   (*c*) Show how the writer's use of imagery in lines 58–61 contributes to your understanding of this line of thought.

   2 A

   (*d*) In lines 65–77, the writer refers to classical statuary and Senator John Glenn as evidence to illustrate his point about how we regard old age nowadays.

   How convincing do you find each of these illustrations? Justify your answers.

   4 A/E

6. By referring to two examples from lines 78–90, show how the writer uses word choice to highlight his feelings about what has happened to old people.

   4 A

7. Show how effective you find the ideas of the final paragraph (lines 91–100) as a conclusion to the passage as a whole.

   4 E

   Questions on Passage 2 (32)

8. From the opening paragraph (lines 1–4) identify **two** ways in which the writer gives the impression that she is addressing the reader directly.

   2 A

9. Explain how the writer defines "growing old disgracefully" in the first sentence of paragraph two (lines 5–7).

   3 U

10. How does the writer use sentence structure and punctuation in lines 18–28 to make clear her point of view?

    4 A/U

11. What might be the question to which "Yes" (line 29) is the answer?

    1 U

12. What is suggested about the writer's relationship with her daughters? You should refer closely to lines 29–41 in your answer.

    4 U/A

13. In the last three paragraphs of the passage (lines 42–69), the writer provides more answers to her original question "How am I growing old disgracefully?" Briefly summarise the main point(s) made in each paragraph.

    6 U

    Questions on both Passages (20)

14. (*a*) Identify the overall tone of each of the passages and say what effect the tone of each had on your appreciation of the passages.

    4 E/A

    (*b*) By close reference to both passages, compare and contrast other aspects of the style of writing of each passage and say how successful you felt each was in conveying the point of view of the writer.

    You should consider such aspects as punctuation, sentence structure, word-choice, use of examples, or any other feature. You must not consider tone.

    4 E/A

    [END OF QUESTION PAPER] (8)

    Total (60)

X039/302

NATIONAL
QUALIFICATIONS
2000

WEDNESDAY, 24 MAY
10.50 AM – 12.20 PM

ENGLISH AND COMMUNICATION
HIGHER
Analysis and Appreciation

There are **two parts** to this paper and you should attempt both parts.

Part 1 (Textual Analysis) is worth 30 marks.

In Part 2 (Critical Essay), you should attempt **one** question only, taken from any of the Sections A–D.

Your answer to Part 2 should begin on a fresh page.

Each question in Part 2 is worth 30 marks.

NB You must not use, in Part 2 of this paper, the same text(s) as you have used in your Specialist Study.

PART 1—TEXTUAL ANALYSIS

Read the following poem and answer the questions which follow.

You are reminded that this part of the paper tests your ability to understand, analyse and evaluate the text.

The number of marks attached to each question will give some indication of the length of answer required.

You should spend about 45 minutes on this part of the paper.

TIMETABLE

We all remember school, of course:
the lino warming, shoe bag smell, expanse
of polished floor. It's where we learned
to wait: hot cheeked in class, dreaming,
5   bored, for cheesy milk, for noisy now.
We learned to count, to rule off days,
and pattern time in coloured squares:
purple English, dark green Maths.

We hear the bells, sometimes,
10   for years, the squeal and crack
of chalk on black. We walk, don't run,
in awkward pairs, hoping for the open door,
a foreign teacher, fire drill. And love
is long aertex summers, tennis sweat,
15   and somewhere, someone singing flat.
The art room, empty, full of light.

Kate Clanchy

QUESTIONS

Marks

1. What effect does "of course" have on your reading of the first line?   **1**

2. Show how the poet evokes a vivid picture of school in lines 2–5.   **4**

3. What attitude about the writer's time in school seems to emerge in lines 6–8? Justify your answer by referring closely to the content and techniques of these lines.   **4**

4. In what way do lines 9–10 link the ideas of verses one and two?   **2**

5. Show how the poet uses sound to enhance the mood in the first sentence of the second verse (lines 9–11).   **4**

6.   ". . . hoping for the open door,
   a foreign teacher, fire drill." (lines 12–13)

   (*a*)   Why might each of these be hoped for?   **3**

   (*b*)   In what way does the idea suggested by these things contrast with
      ". . . We walk, don't run,
      in awkward pairs . . ." (lines 11–12)?   **2**

7. In the final lines, the writer refers to tennis, singing and the art room. What do any **two** of these references contribute to the mood of the final part of the poem?   **4**

8. What do you see as the relationship between the title of the poem and:

   (*a*)   verse one;

   (*b*)   verse two?   **6**

Total (30)

[Turn over for PART 2—CRITICAL ESSAY

PART 2—CRITICAL ESSAY

Attempt ONE question only, taken from any of the Sections A to D. Write the number of the question you attempt in the margin of your answer book.

In all Sections you may use Scottish texts.

You must not use the poem from the Textual Analysis part of the paper as the subject of your Critical Essay.

You are reminded that the quality of your writing and its accuracy are important in this paper as is the relevance of your answer to the question you have attempted.

You should spend about 45 minutes on this part of the paper.

Begin your answer on a fresh page.

SECTION A—DRAMA

1. Choose a play which is based partly or wholly on historical events.

   Discuss to what extent, in your opinion, the play retains its relevance in the modern world.

   In your answer you must refer closely to the text and to at least two of: theme, setting, characterisation, key scene(s), or any other appropriate feature.

2. Choose a play in which the deterioration of a marriage or a relationship is important.

   Show how the dramatist presents the deterioration, and why it is, in your opinion, important to the play as a whole.

   In your answer you must refer closely to the text and to at least two of: characterisation, theme, dialogue, plot, conflict, or any other appropriate feature.

3. Choose a play with a clear political or social or religious message.

   Outline briefly what the "message" is and go on to explain the methods by which the dramatist makes you aware of it.

   In your answer you must refer closely to the text and to at least two of: theme, characterisation, setting, dramatic style, or any other appropriate feature.

4. Choose a play in which one speech or piece of dialogue is particularly important.

   Put the speech or piece of dialogue in context, and then go on to explain why you think it is particularly important to the rest of the play.

   In your answer you must refer closely to the text and to at least two of: characterisation, theme, language, climax, or any other appropriate feature.

SECTION B—PROSE

5. Choose a novel or short story in which an element of mystery plays an important part.

   Show how the development and resolution of the mystery contributed to your enjoyment of the text as a whole.

   In your answer you must refer closely to the text and to at least two of: atmosphere, key incident(s), plot, narrative stance, setting, or any other appropriate feature.

6. Choose a novel which you think has a definite turning point or decisive moment.

   Explain briefly what happens at that point or moment and go on to explain why you think it is so important to the rest of the novel.

   In your answer you must refer closely to the text and to at least two of: key incident(s), structure, plot, theme, characterisation, or any other appropriate feature.

7. Choose a work of non-fiction which had a powerful impact on you.

   Show how the writer managed to achieve this effect.

   In your answer you must refer closely to the text and to at least two of: language, point of view, theme, structure, mood, or any other appropriate feature.

8. Choose a novel or short story in which humour plays an important part.

   Explain how the humour is created and show how it made an important contribution to your enjoyment of the text as a whole.

   In your answer you must refer closely to the text and to at least two of: characterisation, dialogue, key incident(s), style, or any other appropriate feature.

SECTION C—POETRY

(In this section you may not answer using "Timetable" by Kate Clanchy)

9. Choose a poem about old age.

   Explain what impression the poet creates of old age and discuss how effectively the impression is created.

   In your answer you must refer closely to the text and to at least two of: theme, imagery, word choice, structure, mood, or any other appropriate feature.

10. Choose two poems which deal with the same theme.

    By referring to both poems, show which you find more effective in dealing with the theme.

    In your answer you must refer closely to the text and to at least two of: theme, structure, word choice, imagery, or any other appropriate feature.

11. Choose a poem which you think could be described as a "quiet" or a "reflective" poem.

    Show how the poet has achieved this effect and discuss to what extent you find it a suitable way of dealing with the subject matter in the poem.

    In your answer you must refer closely to the text and to at least two of: mood, theme, sound, imagery, rhythm, or any other appropriate feature.

12. Choose a poem with an impressive opening.

    Explain why you think the opening was so impressive and discuss how effectively it prepared you for the rest of the poem.

    In your answer you must refer closely to the text and to at least two of: theme, imagery, sound, development, form, or any other appropriate feature.

[Turn over

SECTION D—MASS MEDIA

13. Choose a film or TV drama which is based partly or wholly on historical events.

Discuss to what extent, in your opinion, the film or TV drama retains its relevance in the modern world.

In your answer you must refer closely to the text and to at least two of: setting, theme, sound track, aspects of mise-en-scène such as costume and objects, or any other appropriate feature.

14. Choose a TV drama or documentary with a clear political or social or religious message.

Outline briefly what the "message" was and go on to explain the methods by which the writer and/or director made you aware of it.

In your answer you must refer closely to the text and to at least two of: theme, point of view, casting, editing, aspects of mise-en-scène such as use of camera, or any other appropriate feature.

15. Choose a film or TV drama in which an element of mystery plays an important part.

Show how the development and resolution of the mystery contributed to your enjoyment of the text as a whole.

In your answer you must refer closely to the text and to at least two of: characterisation, plot, editing, aspects of mise-en-scène such as use of camera and lighting, or any other appropriate feature.

16. Choose a film which you think has a definite turning point or decisive moment.

Explain briefly what happens at that point or moment and go on to explain why you think it is so important to the rest of the film.

In your answer you must refer closely to the text and to at least two of: plot, editing, sound track, aspects of mise-en-scène such as lighting and use of camera, or any other appropriate feature.

[END OF QUESTION PAPER]

2001 HIGHER

X039/301

NATIONAL
QUALIFICATIONS
2001

TUESDAY, 15 MAY
9.00 AM – 10.30 AM

ENGLISH AND COMMUNICATION
HIGHER
Close Reading

You should attempt all questions.

The total value of the Paper is 60 marks.

There are TWO passages and questions.

Read both passages carefully and then answer all the questions which follow. **Use your own words whenever possible and particularly when you are instructed to do so.**

You should read each passage to:

understand what the authors are saying about Muhammed Ali (**Understanding—U**);

analyse their choices of language, imagery and structures to recognise how they convey their points of view and contribute to the impact of the passages (**Analysis—A**);

evaluate how effectively each writer has achieved his purpose (**Evaluation—E**).

A code letter (U, A, E) is used alongside each question to give some indication of the skills being assessed. The number of marks attached to each question will give some indication of the length of answer required.

SCOTTISH
QUALIFICATIONS
AUTHORITY

PASSAGE 1

Journalist, Ian Wooldridge, reflects on the life of Muhammed Ali in an article which appeared in the British Airways magazine High Life *in 2000. It is slightly adapted.*

THE GREATEST VICTIM

I first set eyes on Muhammed Ali in the beautiful Palazzo dello Sport in Rome on a September evening in 1960. His name then was Cassius Clay. He was 18 years old, incredibly handsome, about
5 to fight for the Olympic light-heavyweight title and looked scared of nothing. This was the first of a myriad of misconceptions and contradictions about the extraordinary man, who 40 years later was overwhelmingly voted the greatest sportsman
10 of the 20th century.

The truth was that he was dead scared of flying. Two months earlier, on his way to the U.S. boxing trials, he had been violently buffeted during a turbulent flight across to California. It was the
15 first time he had travelled by air and he swore he would never fly again. This was marginally inconvenient when he was one of the hottest hopes America had for Olympic boxing gold. It took hours of persuasion and cajolery to talk him back
20 on to the plane to Italy.

I have often wondered whether the world would have heard of him had he dug his heels in on the day of departure. Probably not. In 1960, in racist, reactionary, bigoted small-town America, uppity
25 young black men were lucky enough to get one break, let alone two.

Destiny determined otherwise. A legend was in the making. What overwhelms you about this man from such a violent trade are the goodness,
30 sincerity and generosity that have survived a lifetime of controversy, racial hatred, fundamental religious conversion, criminal financial exploitation, marital upheavals, revilement by many of his own nation and, eventually, the
35 collapse of his own body.

Little did I visualise, 37 years after that Roman evening, I would meet him again and be reduced to tears. The supreme athlete and unique showman once deemed by *Time* magazine to be the most
40 instantly recognised human being in the world, struggled up from a settee, tottered unsteadily across the carpet and embraced me in an enveloping bear-hug. Facially bloated, he could speak only in brief, almost unintelligible gasps.
45 Reminiscence was impossible. He smiled a lot, but he suffers from narcolepsy as well as the brain damage which some have identified as Parkinson's disease. Every few minutes he slept while his fourth wife, Lonnie, took over the conversation. A
50 little girl in 1960, living in the same street as the Olympic hero and holding a torch for him, she stepped in thirty years later when, health gone and

asset-stripped by rapacious promoters, he was on the skids.

How did Ali, the icon of world sport, come to this? 55 It was a cavalier attitude to money when it was plentiful, an almost childlike trust in the untrustworthy and, throughout, an utterly reckless generosity. One fight I attended in Kuala Lumpur, Malaysia, showed a fascinating insight 60 into how the money haemorrhaged. He was accompanied by a retinue of 44, of whom perhaps six were professionally involved. The rest were relatives, friends of relatives, old pals of Ali who had fallen on hard times, and outright leeches. 65 Daily they plundered the hotel's shopping mall amassing clothes, jewellery and tacky souvenirs, all charged to Ali's account. But there were also altruistic courtiers. Two days before the fight, I was visited by one Charlie Perkins, an ex-Everton 70 footballer I knew slightly. He is an Australian Aborigine, extremely articulate and an evangelist for Aboriginal rights. Charlie had a simple objective—to persuade Ali to fly down to Australia and throw his personality and enormous influence 75 behind their cause. Ali was sympathetic but, no, he would not proceed to Australia. What he did was to put Perkins (and his companions) on his payroll in some spurious capacity and pick up the tab for their airfares back to Sydney. He never met them again. 80 And mainstream America's rejection? He was a national hero on his return to Louisville from his Olympic triumph, but there were still those who called him "boy" and restaurants which didn't admit blacks. Disillusioned, his riposte was 85 to jettison the name Cassius Clay, handed down from the slave owners of his African forebears, and become Muhammed Ali, pilgrim of Mecca, convert to the Muslim faith. It was a predictable decision but one which was to bring opprobrium 90 upon him nationwide. To much of middle-class America he was now a renegade and soon became a pariah when he refused the draft to fight for his country in Vietnam. "I ain't got no quarrel with them Vietcong," he said, and was subsequently, at the 95 peak of his career, banned from boxing for four years.

I am not a boxing expert. Those who are, mostly endorse Muhammed Ali's opinion of himself at his peak: "The Greatest." But it took a long time for 100 mainstream America to become reconciled to that judgement. For many, he was a turbulent, disturbing figure who challenged homespun values.

105 But then eventually there came a night when he won over most of the remaining doubters. It was the best kept secret of the 1996 Olympic Games in Atlanta, at the very heart of America's Deep South, when he emerged high in the tower of the stadium, to extend
110 a trembling arm and apply, just, a flaming torch to light the Olympic cauldron.

Three years later, he was honoured as the Sports Personality of the Millennium, and we held our breath as he struggled with a few words to an
115 adoring audience. The following evening at a dinner, I sat next to him. Having met everyone in the room, he slumbered throughout most of the proceedings. But I had learned to cope with it now, knowing that in his waking moments he could understand everything you said while unable to reply 120 coherently. I had left a pen lying on the table. Ali picked it up and began to doodle on the linen cloth with nursery drawings. "Skyscraper," he whispered. "Airplane." There were six or seven of them and when he'd finished we whipped the cloth from the 125 table and auctioned it on the spot for £10,300 for charity. Muhammed Ali beamed at that. The man who had let millions slip through his fingers knew he was still helping those even less fortunate than himself. 130

PASSAGE 2

The passage is adapted from the introduction to I'm a Little Special—a Muhammed Ali Reader. *Gerald Early considers his feelings in the 1960s about his boyhood hero.*

THE GREAT ALI

I was no good at wood-working and the like, so I saved my paper route money, and simply bought a baseball bat, a genuine Louisville Slugger, the first one I ever owned. I sanded that bat, re-stained it
5 dark, gave it a name. I carved, scratched really, into the bat the word, *Ali.* I tried to carve a lightning bolt but my limited artistic skill would not permit it. I wanted to carry it in a case but I didn't have one. I just slung it over my shoulder like the great
10 weapon it was, my knight's sword. And I felt like some magnificent knight, some great protector of honour and virtue, whenever I walked on the field.

I used that bat the entire summer and a magical season it was. I was the best hitter in the
15 neighbourhood. Once, I won a game in the last at-bat with a home run, and the boys just crowded round me as if I were a spectacle to behold, as if I were, for some small moment, in this insignificant part of the world, playing this meaningless game,
20 their majestic, golden prince.

But, the bat broke. Some kid used it without my permission. He hit a foul ball and the bat split, the barrel flying away, the splintered handle still in the kid's hands.

25 That was 1966 and Muhammed Ali seemed not simply the best boxer of the day but the best boxer who could possibly be imagined—so good that it was an inspiration to see even a picture of him. My body shivered when I saw him as if an electric shock
30 had pulverised my ability to feel. No fighter could touch him. His self-knowledge was glorious, so transcendently fixed was he on the only two subjects he knew: himself and boxing. He so filled me with his holy spirit that whenever, late in a game, our side needed a rally, I would call out Ali's 35 chant to my teammates, "Float like a butterfly sting like a bee!" That made little sense metaphorically in relation to baseball, but it seemed to work more often than not. It was for me, the summer of 1966, Ali's absolute moment of 40 black possibilities fulfilled. And I wanted that and had it for a moment, too, had it, perhaps, among the neighbourhood guys, the touch and glory of the great Ali.

When the bat broke, it seemed a certain spell was 45 broken, too. I drifted away from baseball by steps and bounds. The next summer, 1967, Ali was convicted of draft-dodging. Martin Luther King came out against the Vietnam War. Baseball did not seem very important. Something else was. For you 50 see, I could never be sure, before that spring when Ali first refused to be drafted, if in the end he really would refuse an unjust fight. So when he did finally refuse, I felt something greater than pride: I felt as though my honour as a black boy had been 55 defended, my honour as a human being. He was the grand knight, after all, the dragon-slayer. And I felt myself, little inner-city boy that I was, his apprentice to the grand imagination, the grand daring. The day that Ali refused the draft, I cried in 60 my room. I cried for him and for myself, for my future and his, for all our black possibilities. If only I could sacrifice like that, I thought. If only I could sacrifice my life like Muhammed Ali . . .

Questions on Passage 1

	Marks	Code

1. (*a*) By referring to lines 1–6 ("I first . . . scared of nothing."), briefly explain two things which attracted the writer to Cassius Clay. Use your own words as far as possible in your answer. — 2 — U

(*b*) Briefly explain the "first" (line 6) contradiction about Cassius Clay referred to in lines 6–11 ("This was . . . of flying."). — 1 — U

(*c*) "This was marginally inconvenient . . . boxing gold." (lines 16–18)

What tone is adopted by the writer in this sentence? Go on to explain briefly how effective you find this tone in the context. — 2 — A/E

2. Look at lines 21–35.

(*a*) Explain what the writer means by "Destiny determined otherwise." (line 27) — 2 — U

(*b*) Show how the writer uses sentence structure in lines 21–35 to dramatise his view about destiny and Muhammed Ali. — 4 — A

3. By referring to lines 36–44, show how the writer uses contrast to convey his shock at meeting Muhammed Ali years later. — 2 — A

4. (*a*) Explain in your own words two reasons for Muhammed Ali's poverty. In your answer, you should refer to lines 55–59 ("How did . . . reckless generosity."). — 2 — U

(*b*) Show how effective you find the writer's use of imagery to convey his feelings about what happened to Muhammed Ali's money. In your answer, you should analyse two examples from lines 59–68 ("One fight . . . Ali's account."). — 4 — A/E

(*c*) What makes Charlie Perkins's motives different from those of Ali's other "courtiers" (line 69)? — 2 — U

5. Summarise the main reasons for "mainstream America's rejection" of Muhammed Ali. You should refer to lines 81–104 in your answer and use your own words as far as possible. — 5 — U

6. Show how **either** of the final two paragraphs effectively illustrates both the "triumph" and the "tragedy" of Muhammed Ali. You should refer to content and style in your answer. — 4 — A/E

(30)

Questions on Passage 2

7. (*a*) By referring to lines 1–8 ("I was . . . have one."), briefly explain how any two of the writer's actions show the importance of the baseball bat to him. — 2 — U

(*b*) Show how the writer uses imagery in lines 9–20 ("I just . . . golden prince.") to convey how the bat affected the way he thought about himself. You should refer to two examples in your answer. — 4 — A

8. Show how the writer's language in lines 21–24 conveys the impact of the destruction of his bat. — 2 — A

9. By referring to lines 25–44, show how the writer uses word choice to convey the intensity of his feelings about Muhammed Ali. — 4 — A

10. (*a*) By referring to the final paragraph (line 45 to the end) explain fully why Muhammed Ali's refusal to fight in the Vietnam War was so significant to the writer. — 4 — U

(*b*) Show how the writer's language in the final paragraph conveys the passion he felt about Ali's decision not to fight in the Vietnam War. In your answer, you should refer to more than one of the following: imagery, sentence structure, punctuation, word choice. — 4 — A

(20)

Questions on both Passages

11. (*a*) From your reading of both passages, what do you think are the key reasons for Muhammed Ali's "greatness"? — 5 — U

(*b*) Which writer's style do you prefer?

Justify your view by referring to both passages and to such features as structure, anecdote, symbolism, imagery, word choice . . . — 5 — A/E

[END OF QUESTION PAPER]

Total (60)

X039/302

NATIONAL
QUALIFICATIONS
2001

TUESDAY, 15 MAY
10.50 AM – 12.20 PM

ENGLISH AND
COMMUNICATION
HIGHER
Analysis and Appreciation

There are **two parts** to this paper and you should attempt both parts.

Part 1 (Textual Analysis) is worth 30 marks.

In Part 2 (Critical Essay), you should attempt **one** question only, taken from any of the Sections A–D.

Your answer to Part 2 should begin on a fresh page.

Each question in Part 2 is worth 30 marks.

NB You must not use, in Part 2 of this paper, the same text(s) as you have used in your Specialist Study.

SCOTTISH
QUALIFICATIONS
AUTHORITY

PART 1—TEXTUAL ANALYSIS

Read the following poem and answer the questions which follow.

You are reminded that this part of the paper tests your ability to understand, analyse and evaluate the text.

The number of marks attached to each question will give some indication of the length of answer required.

You should spend about 45 minutes on this part of the paper.

In this poem "Originally" by Carol Ann Duffy, the initial situation seems to picture a family journey or move from one town to another.

ORIGINALLY

We came from our own country in a red room
which fell through the fields, our mother singing
our father's name to the turn of the wheels.
My brothers cried, one of them bawling *Home,*
5   *Home*, as the miles rushed back to the city,
the street, the house, the vacant rooms
where we didn't live any more. I stared
at the eyes of a blind toy, holding its paw.

All childhood is an emigration. Some are slow,
10   leaving you standing, resigned, up an avenue
where no one you know stays. Others are sudden.
Your accent wrong. Corners, which seem familiar,
leading to unimagined, pebble-dashed estates, big boys
eating worms and shouting words you don't understand.
15   My parents' anxiety stirred like a loose tooth
in my head. *I want our own country*, I said.

But then you forget, or don't recall, or change,
and, seeing your brother swallow a slug, feel only
a skelf of shame. I remember my tongue
20   shedding its skin like a snake, my voice
in the classroom sounding just like the rest. Do I only think
I lost a river, culture, speech, sense of first space
and the right place? Now, *Where do you come from?*
strangers ask. *Originally?* And I hesitate.

Carol Ann Duffy

QUESTIONS

Marks

1. (*a*) The poet seems to be moving to a different part of the country. What do you think is the mood in the first three lines of the poem? Briefly justify your answer.

   2

   (*b*) Explain in detail how a contrast is created between the poet and her brothers in the rest of verse one (lines 4–8).

   3

2. (*a*) "All childhood is an emigration." (line 9)

   What do you think this line means?

   2

   (*b*) "Some are slow," (line 9) "Others are sudden" (line 11).

   Show how the poet highlights features of each emigration in lines 9–14. You should refer to word choice, sentence structure and sound in your answer.

   6

3. "My parents' anxiety stirred like a loose tooth in my head. *I want our own country*, I said." (lines 15–16)

   (*a*) Why might the parents be anxious?

   1

   (*b*) How effective do you find the image in this context (lines 15–16)?

   2

4. Explain how the language of lines 17–21 helps you to appreciate the change introduced by the word "But".

   4

5. How do the ideas of the last section of the poem from "Do I only . . ." (line 21 to the end) justify the choice of "Originally" as the title of the poem?

   4

6. What do you think is an important theme in this poem? How effectively do you feel the poem has explored this theme?

   You may wish to consider such language features as imagery, tone, point of view, enjambement, structure of the poem . . .

   6

   (30)

[Turn over for PART 2—CRITICAL ESSAY

PART 2—CRITICAL ESSAY

Attempt ONE question only, taken from any of the Sections A to D. Write the number of the question you attempt in the margin of your answer book.

In all Sections you may use Scottish texts.

You must not use the poem from the Textual Analysis part of the paper as the subject of your Critical Essay.

You are reminded that the quality of your writing and its accuracy are important in this paper as is the relevance of your answer to the question you have attempted.

You should spend about 45 minutes on this part of the paper.

Begin your answer on a fresh page.

SECTION A—DRAMA

1. Choose a play in which a character makes a brave decision.

    Briefly explain the circumstances which lead up to the decision and then discuss how it affects your views of the character.

    In your answer you must refer closely to the text and to at least two of: characterisation, key scene, theme, dialogue, or any other appropriate feature.

2. Choose a play whose main theme you feel is important to you personally.

    Show how the dramatist explores the theme and discuss to what extent the play influenced your views.

    In your answer you must refer closely to the text and to at least two of: theme, setting, conflict, key scene(s), or any other appropriate feature.

3. Choose from a play a scene in which one character makes an accusation against another character.

    Explain the dramatic importance of the scene and discuss how it affects your sympathy for either or both of the characters.

    In your answer you must refer closely to the text and to at least two of: dialogue, key scene, characterisation, theme, or any other appropriate feature.

4. Choose from a play a scene in which you felt totally involved (either as an audience member at a performance, or as a reader).

    Show how the skill of the dramatist or of those making the performance caused you to be so involved.

    In your answer you must refer closely to the text and to at least two of: theme, characterisation, stage directions, aspects of staging such as lighting, sound, movement, costume, or any other appropriate feature.

glass menagrie

SECTION B—PROSE

5. Choose a novel which explores the nature of evil.

Show how the writer's exploration of the theme enhanced your understanding of evil.

In your answer you must refer closely to the text and to at least two of: theme, setting, symbolism, characterisation, or any other appropriate feature.

6. Choose a novel or short story in which the method of narration makes a major contribution to its impact.

Describe the method of narration and explain why you feel it makes a major contribution to your appreciation of the text as a whole.

In your answer you must refer closely to the text and to at least two of: narrative technique, theme, language, structure, or any other appropriate feature.

7. Choose a **non-fiction text** in which the writer's attention to detail is an important factor.

Illustrate the writer's skill in this area and explain why you feel it makes a major contribution to your appreciation of the text as a whole.

In your answer you must refer closely to the text and to at least two of: style, ideas, point of view, setting, anecdote, or any other appropriate feature.

8. Choose a novel or short story which is set in the past.

Discuss to what extent, despite the distance in time, you were engaged by the actions and beliefs of one of the characters.

In your answer you must refer closely to the text and to at least two of: setting, characterisation, key incident(s), theme, or any other appropriate feature.

SECTION C—POETRY

In this Section you may not answer using "Originally" by Carol Ann Duffy

9. Choose a poem which creates a sense of menace.

Show how the poet achieves this and discuss how it adds to your appreciation of the poem.

In your answer you must refer closely to the text and to at least two of: mood, theme, imagery, sound, or any other appropriate feature.

10. Choose a poem on the subject of love.

Show how the poet treats the subject, and explain to what extent you find the treatment convincing.

In your answer you must refer closely to the text and to at least two of: theme, imagery, form, tone, or any other appropriate feature.

11. Choose a poet who reflects on the idea of change.

Show how the poet explores the subject in one or more of his/her poems, and explain to what extent your appreciation of the subject was deepened.

In your answer you must refer closely to the text and to at least two of: theme, structure, imagery, tone, or any other appropriate feature.

12. Choose a poem which is written in a specific poetic form, such as dramatic monologue, sonnet, ode, ballad.

Show how the particular form helped your appreciation of the ideas and/or feelings which the poem explores.

In your answer you must refer closely to the text and to at least two of: form, theme, rhythm and rhyme, imagery, or any other appropriate feature.

[Turn over

SECTION D—MASS MEDIA

13. Choose a film or TV drama* in which a character makes a brave decision.

    Briefly explain the circumstances which lead up to the decision and then discuss how it affects our views of the character.

    In your answer you must refer closely to the text and to at least two of: key scene, dialogue, casting, aspects of mise-en-scène such as lighting and use of camera, or any other appropriate feature.

14. Choose a TV drama* whose main theme you feel is important to you personally.

    Show how the dramatist explores the theme and discuss to what extent the text influenced your views.

    In your answer you must refer closely to the text and to at least two of: theme, setting, conflict, montage, sound, or any other appropriate feature.

15. Choose a film or TV drama* which is set in the past.

    Discuss to what extent, despite the distance in time, you were engaged by the actions and beliefs of one of the characters.

    In your answer you must refer closely to the text and to at least two of: setting, characterisation, key sequence(s), aspects of mise-en-scène such as costume and props, or any other appropriate feature.

16. Choose a film which creates a sense of menace.

    Show how the film-makers achieve this and discuss how it adds to your appreciation of the film.

    In your answer you must refer closely to the text and to at least two of: mood, montage, sound, aspects of mise-en-scène such as lighting and use of camera, or any other appropriate feature.

*"TV drama" may be a single play, series or serial.

[END OF QUESTION PAPER]

X039/301

NATIONAL
QUALIFICATIONS
2002

THURSDAY, 16 MAY
9.00 AM – 10.30 AM

ENGLISH AND COMMUNICATION

HIGHER

Close Reading

You should attempt all questions.

The total value of the Paper is 50 marks.

There are TWO passages and questions.

Read both passages carefully and then answer all the questions which follow. **Use your own words whenever possible and particularly when you are instructed to do so.**

You should read each passage to:

understand what the authors are saying about music (**Understanding—U**);

analyse their choices of language, imagery and structures to recognise how they convey their points of view and contribute to the impact of the passages (**Analysis—A**);

evaluate how effectively each writer has achieved his purpose (**Evaluation—E**).

A code letter (U, A, E) is used alongside each question to give some indication of the skills being assessed. The number of marks attached to each question will give some indication of the length of answer required.

SCOTTISH
QUALIFICATIONS
AUTHORITY

PASSAGE 1

The passage is adapted from Big Bangs—The Story of Five Discoveries that Changed Musical History *by Howard Goodall. In this passage, the writer considers the impact of being able to record music.*

We are sitting at one end of a time corridor, over a thousand years long. We, that is you and I, are trying to concentrate on the dark remoteness at the other end—the Dark Ages of Europe. They, the
5 foreigners at the other end, are almost silent. Whilst we are bathed in light and colour, they are hiding from the harsh glare of the sun in what looks like a cell or a tunnel. To us they seem like children in many ways, with their Nativity stories, ghosts
10 and miracles, their unquestioning beliefs and their Gardens of Eden. If they could see us, they would think us indescribably rich and exotic.

At our end of the corridor there is a musical cacophony, at theirs a profound and disheartening
15 silence. At our end of the corridor there are a thousand different voices demanding to be heard, demanding our attention. Music has become more than a backdrop—it has become a blaring soundtrack for practically every event in our lives,
20 whether we are travelling, eating, shopping, exercising, making love or being cremated. We are even given music to "listen to" in the womb. Knowledge and information overwhelm us. At their cold and gloomy end of the corridor,
25 however, only a trickle of learning and culture survives from classical times, mainly through hearsay and deduction.

They have all but lost the flow of the blood of music. It has become for them a distant,
30 heartbreaking echo, surviving only in the keening lamentation of what will one day be known as "Gregorian" plainsong. This, the mother of our music, inherited rough-edged from the Jews, then smoothed into a musical marble, a last mournful
35 relic of centuries of joyful exuberance, is their solace in the medieval gloom. Every single note of the music of Imperial Rome, in the absence of some form of notation, has been lost. What writing is to language, notation is to music. The survival
40 without notation of something quite so delicate as Gregorian plainsong through hundreds of years of war, invasion and pestilence is nothing short of miraculous.

I am a composer. Not an important one, but one
45 who feels nevertheless some kind of ancient, almost mystical gratitude to a humble monk, at the other end of this millennial corridor. Guido Monaco, Guido "the monk", was a jobbing musical director at a cathedral church in what is
50 now called Tuscany in the early years of the eleventh century. He was charged with the task of teaching the choristers the chants which formed the backbone of the worship of that period. To my mind, Guido is no less important than Beethoven

or Presley, Wagner or the Beatles. He is the father 55 and facilitator of every note they wrote. He gave us our system of musical notation. Guido taught us how we might write our music down. His solution—worried out of a bewildering chaos of possibilities, like precious metal from ore—has 60 served us unswervingly for a thousand years. I am peering into his empty room, his silent almost music-less world at the place and time of the birth of recorded music in Western Europe.

Our gaze now shifts much nearer in the time 65 corridor—to the invention of recorded sound. Though the early gramophone came into being in the 1870s as a result of the desire to record and reproduce speech, very soon its principal, almost monogamous marriage was with music. Thomas 70 Alva Edison's invention of recorded sound unleashed on the twentieth century a massive amount of music in a multitude of forms; it gave music wings to cross the planet. Before the gramophone age, people heard a particular piece of 75 orchestral music maybe once or twice a *decade*. Now anything can be listened to, instantly, at the flick of a switch, the drop of a needle or the aiming of a laser. 150 years ago the very slowness of making a notated score of a piece of music meant 80 that the creator had to live with it and think about it for a period of time before it was released to the world. Now a recording can be made instantaneously, even at the point of creation. Where once a catchy, impulsive melody made up 85 on the spot and enjoyed for the evening would die the next morning, never to be heard again, now everything can be captured for posterity. And in addition, where once musicians lived and died on their live performance, now editing allows them to 90 relive and redo their mistakes and wobbles as many times as they like.

The ability to record sound has had a profound, irreversible effect on music and what we as listeners expect from it. A battle has been created 95 between the concept of music as a living, breathing, organic "condition", ceaselessly reinventing and reprocessing itself, never static, never finished, and the concept of music as a perfect thing, frozen in time like a painting, 100 sculpture, poem or building. At our music-filled end of the time corridor, have we come to love the perfect copy a little too much? Are we more at ease with the reproduction than the genuine live experience, warts and all? Has recording spoilt us 105 and numbed us to the excitement and drama of the Real Thing?

PASSAGE 2

The passage is adapted from Lost in Music *by Giles Smith. It is 1972 and the author's two older brothers, Simon and Jeremy, take him (at the age of ten) to see the first live performance of* Relic, *the band in which they are drummer and lead guitarist.*

Odd, this business of going out to "see" a band. My parents, when they were younger, would probably have talked about going to hear a band or going to dance to one, and would not have recognised or
5 understood the ritual that evolved with rock: clumps of people solemnly gathering to face the stage.

Lexden Church Hall was a typical modern municipal amenity: orange and green curtains, a
10 squeaky floor and a faint smell of hospitals. To encourage an atmosphere, most of the lights were off. Eventually, a light came on, revealing Jeremy, stamping on a distortion pedal and churning out a monstrous riff, dimly discernible as the opening to
15 "Paranoid" by Black Sabbath.
BLAN, BLAN, BLAN, DIDDLE-DIDDLE-DIDDLE-DIDDLE
BLAN, BLAN, BLAN, DIDDLE-DIDDLE-DIDDLE-DIDDLE
20 Then some more lights came on and the whole band piled in.

I had stood up when the curtains parted but was nearly forced to sit down again by a sickening combination of excitement and fear, which I was to
25 re-experience not long after this at Ipswich stock car stadium, watching a friend of the family compete in a hot-rod race.

Relic crashed through "Long Train Running" by the Doobie Brothers. They thundered into
30 "Locomotive Breath" by Jethro Tull. The evening offered more than a bit part for Fred the roadie. He scuttled on, two minutes in and every three minutes thereafter, bent over at the waist in approved roadie style, to carry out running repairs on the fatigued
35 metal of Simon's drum kit, nobly ducking the bits of splintered drumstick and the hot cymbal shards as he worked.

No one had the confidence to move around during the songs, except the singer, who had confidence to
40 spare. He wore a body-hugging scoop-necked T-shirt and a pair of white trousers as tight in the groin as they were loose at the ankles. He seemed to have learned by heart the *Bumper Book of Mikestand Manoeuvres*. He lifted its circular weighted
45 base off the floor and toted the stand like a barge pole, in the manner of Rod Stewart; he hopped across the boards, towing it behind him; he forced it down towards the stage in an aggressive tango; he howled into the microphone and then thrust it away
50 to arm's length. Only the low ceiling prevented him from slinging the thing skywards. During instrumental passages, he maintained his place at centre stage, mouth open, nostrils flared, shaking his long blond hair, clapping in time, posturing
55 madly. It was an utterly commanding performance—the performance of a man who knew exactly whose show it was. Accordingly, shortly after this gig, the band voted to replace him with someone much calmer, who came on in a nine-foot
60 scarf and mostly stood at the mike smoking.

At five-second intervals, I glanced down the hall to see what effect all this was having on the audience. It was having very little. The place was about a quarter full. But there were three or four girls at the
65 front watching intently. They looked on gooey-eyed at this frank display of white loon pants and cheap electric guitars.

Near the end of Relic's allotted twenty minutes, Simon closed "Honky Tonk Women"
70 with a magnificent final flourish. Sadly there was still a verse to go. Everybody else, catching the imperative force of that last, juddering drum figure, had come to a halt with him. There was a pause, probably only a couple of seconds long, but
75 suddenly time felt heavy as lead. Relic exchanged bewildered looks. I felt as if I was about to throw up. But then, like the cavalry regrouping, they set off once more, ground their way back up to speed, beat a path through the final
80 verse and ended again, Simon's flourish sounding a little more sheepish this time. After that, they were gone. And no encores.

I lay in bed that night with singed ears. With hindsight, it has occurred to me that Relic were really, by default, Colchester's first punk band,
85 breathtakingly meritless. But I didn't think about that then. I thought about the noise, the lights, the leaping around. I thought about the gooey-eyed girls. I thought I could see a way forward.

Questions on Passage 1   *Marks*   *Code*

1. Consider lines 1–12.

   (*a*) Using your own words as far as possible, identify **two** ways in which the world of "the Dark Ages of Europe" (line 4) was different from ours.   2   **U**

   (*b*) Show how the writer's word choice in these lines illuminates any **two** aspects of either our world or theirs.   4   **A**

2. (*a*) "At our end . . . silence." (lines 13–15)

   Using your own words as far as possible, explain the meaning of this sentence.   2   **U**

   (*b*) Show how the writer's sentence structure and imagery emphasise the contrasting musical environments of people in the Dark Ages and people today. You should refer to lines 13–27 in your answer.   4   **A**

3. Consider lines 28–43.

   (*a*) Explain briefly the importance of Gregorian plainsong:

      (i)   in the lives of the Dark Ages people;   1   **U**

      (ii) to the music of our times.   1   **U**

   (*b*) Explain briefly **two** reasons why the survival of Gregorian plainsong is "nothing short of miraculous" (lines 42–43).   2   **U**

4. Consider lines 44–64.

   (*a*) Explain why, according to the writer, people today should feel gratitude towards Guido Monaco.   2   **U**

   (*b*) Show how the writer's language highlights the importance of what Guido Monaco did. You should refer to **one** technique in your answer.   2   **A**

5. Consider lines 65–92.

   Using your own words as far as possible, identify **five** benefits the gramophone has brought to the world of music.   5   **U**

6. (*a*) Using your own words as far as possible, explain the "battle" (line 95) described by the writer in lines 93–107.   2   **U**

   (*b*) In lines 101–107, the writer poses three questions. What do you think his answer would be to each of these questions? Justify your view in each case by referring briefly to the language of each question.   3   **A**

                                                                (30)

Questions on Passage 2

7. Explain the significance of the word "ritual" (line 5) in the context of lines 1–7.   2   **U**

8. Consider lines 8–37.

   Show how the writer conveys his feelings about the whole experience described in these lines. In your answer you may refer to tone, point of view, onomatopoeia, imagery, or any other appropriate language feature.   4   **A**

9. Consider lines 38–60.

   (*a*) Which contributes more to the writer's presentation of the singer: **word choice** or **sentence structure**? Justify your choice by referring closely to both of these features.   4   **A/E**

   (*b*) Identify the tone of lines 57–60 ("Accordingly . . . at the mike smoking").   1   **A**

10. "breathtakingly meritless" (line 86)

   By referring to lines 61–82, explain fully what justification the writer has for making this comment about Relic.   3   **U**

                                                                (14)

Question on both Passages

11. Which passage did you find more stimulating?

   In your answer you should refer to the styles and to the ideas of both passages. You may make reference to material you have used in earlier answers.   6   **E**

[END OF QUESTION PAPER]

                                                                    Total (50)

X039/302

NATIONAL
QUALIFICATIONS
2002

THURSDAY, 16 MAY
10.50 AM – 12.20 PM

ENGLISH AND
COMMUNICATION
HIGHER
Analysis and Appreciation

There are **two parts** to this paper and you should attempt both parts.

Part 1 (Textual Analysis) is worth 30 marks.

In Part 2 (Critical Essay), you should attempt **one** question only, taken from any of the Sections A–D.

Your answer to Part 2 should begin on a fresh page.

Each question in Part 2 is worth 30 marks.

NB You must not use, in Part 2 of this paper, the same text(s) as you have used in your Specialist Study.

SCOTTISH
QUALIFICATIONS
AUTHORITY

©

PART 1—TEXTUAL ANALYSIS

Read the following passage and answer the questions which follow.

You are reminded that this part of the paper tests your ability to understand, analyse and evaluate the text.

The number of marks attached to each question will give some indication of the length of answer required.

You should spend about 45 minutes on this part of the paper.

The following passage is about the writer's visit to see "The Jaguar Throne" which is inside a pyramid at Chichen Itza, a site of ancient Mayan civilisation in Mexico.

The Jaguar Throne

We're standing in line to see the Jaguar Throne. It's almost Christmas now and everything is crowded, including the monasteries converted to ten-dollar-a-room hotels and the washrooms
5 crammed with feet, in pastel sandals and the smell of orange peels and other things, and the crumbling hilltop temples with their inner walls luxuriant with graffiti, but this is the last chance we may ever have. Who knows when we'll be
10 passing this way again?

The Jaguar Throne is embedded in a pyramid. First you go through a narrow tunnel entered at ground level, a tunnel so narrow your shoulders touch each side, the old stone unpleasantly
15 damp, with a skin on it like the skin on a stagnant pond. There is only one passageway. Those who have already seen the Jaguar Throne push past us on the way back, squeezing us against the skin of the wall, in their hurry to
20 reach the outside air again. Eagerly we scan their faces: was it worth it?

There are a few small lightbulbs strung along the ceiling, a wire festooned between them. The ceiling itself is getting lower. The air is moist
25 and dead. The line inches forward. Ahead of us there are backs, the necks sunburned, the shirts and dresses ringed with sweat beneath the arms. Nobody says anything, though the heavy air seems full of whispers. Ahead of us, up some
30 steps, around corners unseen, the Jaguar Throne crouches in a square cubicle, its ruby eyes glowing, its teeth vivid, its meaning lost. Who used it last, what was it for, why was it kept here, out of sight in the darkness?

35 The line of people moves forward into the absence of light. There must have been processions once, flames carried, dimming in the lack of oxygen, men in masks, willing or not. The Jaguar Throne was not always a curiosity,
40 something to see at Christmas. Once there were gods who needed propitiation. Once they played a game here, in an outside court, with stone rings set into the walls. If your team lost they cut off your head. That's what the carving
45 is, the body of a man with a fountain in place of the head: the blessed loser, making it rain. Metaphor can be dangerous. Not everyone wants to see the Jaguar Throne but some see it anyway.

50 Ahead of us a woman screams. Panic runs through the line, you can feel it jumping from body to body, there's a surge backwards: in a minute we'll be stampeded, crushed. Then comes the rumour, the whisper: it was only a
55 spider. We're caught anyway, the tunnel's jammed, we can't move, we stand in the dead air listening to our hearts, and now we know the answer: the Jaguar Throne is kept in here so it can't get out.

Margaret Atwood

QUESTIONS

Marks

1. (*a*) What mood or atmosphere do you think is created in lines 1–10?

    1

   (*b*) Show how this mood or atmosphere is created. In your answer you should refer to at least two techniques such as word choice, tone, sentence structure.

    4

2. Read lines 11–21.

   (*a*) Explain fully how the language of these lines makes the experience described seem unpleasant.

    4

   (*b*) Show how effective you find the last sentence "Eagerly we scan . . ." as a conclusion to the paragraph.

    2

3. (*a*) Select one detail from the description in lines 22–29 ("There are a few . . . full of whispers.") and show how it creates an oppressive or a claustrophobic mood.

    2

   (*b*) In what ways do sentence structure and imagery in lines 29–34 contribute to the mysterious nature of the Jaguar Throne?

    4

4. (*a*) By referring to lines 35–49, briefly describe three key features of the rituals associated with the Jaguar Throne. Use your own words as far as possible.

    3

   (*b*) Explain what you think "Metaphor can be dangerous" (line 47) means in the context of lines 43–46.

    2

5. Explain how the language of the final paragraph (lines 50–59) develops the crowd's sense of panic. In your answer you should refer to techniques such as sentence structure, imagery, punctuation, word-choice . . .

    4

6. "the Jaguar Throne is kept in here so it can't get out." (lines 58–59)

   By referring to the passage as a whole, explain why you think the narrator draws this conclusion about the significance of the Jaguar Throne.

    4

    (30)

[Turn over for PART 2—CRITICAL ESSAY

PART 2—CRITICAL ESSAY

Attempt ONE question only, taken from any of the Sections A to D. Write the number of the question you attempt in the margin of your answer book.

In all Sections you may use Scottish texts.

You must not use the extract from the Textual Analysis part of the paper as the subject of your Critical Essay.

You are reminded that the quality of your writing and its accuracy are important in this paper as is the relevance of your answer to the question you have attempted.

You should spend about 45 minutes on this part of the paper.

Begin your answer on a fresh page.

SECTION A—DRAMA

1. Choose a play in which a character struggles with her or his conscience.

    Outline briefly the reasons for the character's dilemma and go on to discuss how successfully the dramatist engages your sympathy for her or him.

    In your answer you must refer closely to the text and to at least two of: characterisation, conflict, theme, resolution, or any other appropriate feature.

2. Choose from a play a scene in which the conflict between two characters is at its most intense.

    Outline briefly the reasons for the conflict and then by examining the scene in detail, show how it gave you a deeper appreciation of the play as a whole.

    In your answer you must refer closely to the text and to at least two of: key scene, dialogue, characterisation, structure, or any other appropriate feature.

3. Choose a play whose main theme concerns one of the following: power, corruption, disillusionment.

    Explain how the dramatist introduces the theme and discuss to what extent you found the way it is explored in the play enhanced your understanding of the theme.

    In your answer you must refer closely to the text and to at least two of: theme, plot, setting, characterisation, or any other appropriate feature.

4. Choose a play in which the main character is at odds with one or more than one of the people around him or her.

    Show how the dramatist makes you aware of the character's situation and discuss to what extent this led to a greater understanding of the concerns of the play.

    In your answer you must refer closely to the text and to at least two of: conflict, characterisation, theme, setting, or any other appropriate feature.

SECTION B—PROSE

(In this Section you may not answer using "The Jaguar Throne" by Margaret Atwood.)

5. Choose a **novel or short story** in which the main character faces a dilemma.

   Outline briefly what the dilemma is and go on to discuss how the character's reaction to it gives you a deeper understanding of the text as a whole.

   In your answer you must refer closely to the text and to at least two of: theme, structure, setting, characterisation, or any other appropriate feature.

6. Choose a **novel** which explores in an effective way a theme which is important to you.

   Explain how the novelist introduces and develops the theme and show to what extent she or he has effectively engaged your interest in it.

   In your answer you must refer closely to the text and to at least two of: theme, structure, setting, symbolism, or any other appropriate feature.

7. Choose a **novel** in which a main character is seen to grow or mature in the course of the story.

   Show how the novelist engages your interest in the character and his or her development.

   In your answer you must refer closely to the text and to at least two of: characterisation, narrative point of view, key incident(s), structure, or any other appropriate feature.

8. Choose a **novel or short story** which has a particularly effective or arresting opening.

   Referring in detail to the opening, discuss to what extent it provides a successful introduction to the text as a whole.

   In your answer you must refer closely to the text and to at least two of: structure, mood, theme, characterisation, or any other appropriate feature.

9. Choose a work of **non-fiction** in which setting in time and/or place is significant.

   Explain why you think the setting is important for your appreciation of the text.

   In your answer you must refer closely to the text and to at least two of: setting, theme, style, descriptive detail, or any other relevant feature.

SECTION C—POETRY

10. Choose a poem in which contrast is used in order to clarify a key idea.

    Examine in detail the poet's use of contrast and show how it was effective in clarifying this key idea.

    In your answer you must refer closely to the text and to at least two of: theme, structure, imagery, sound, or any other appropriate feature.

11. Choose a poet who reflects on the power, the beauty or the threat of the natural world.

    Referring to one or more poems, show how effectively you think the poet explores her or his main idea(s).

    In your answer you must refer closely to the text and to at least two of: mood, imagery, symbolism, sound, or any other appropriate feature.

12. Choose a poem which explores one of the following: freedom, friendship, happiness.

    Discuss to what extent the poem successfully engages your interest in this main idea.

    In your answer you must refer closely to the text and to at least two of: theme, tone, word choice, rhythm, or any other appropriate feature.

13. Choose a poem which presents a character who provokes you to contempt or anger or irritation.

    Show how the poet arouses this response from you and discuss how important it is to the overall impact of the poem.

    In your answer you must refer closely to the text and to at least two of: tone, characterisation, verse form, point of view, or any other appropriate feature.

SECTION D—MASS MEDIA

14. Choose a film which has a particularly effective or arresting opening.

    Referring in detail to the opening, discuss to what extent it provides a successful introduction to the text as a whole.

    In your answer you must refer closely to the text and to at least two of: aspects of mise-en-scène, structure, editing, soundtrack, or any other appropriate feature.

15. Choose from a film or TV drama* a scene in which the conflict between two characters is at its most intense.

    Outline briefly the reasons for the conflict and then by examining the scene in detail, show how it gave you a deeper appreciation of the text as a whole.

    In your answer you must refer closely to the text and to at least two of: key scene, characterisation, dialogue, aspects of mise-en-scène, or any other appropriate feature.

16. Choose a TV drama* in which the character struggles with her or his conscience.

    Outline briefly the reasons for the character's dilemma and go on to discuss how successfully the programme-makers engage your sympathy for her or him.

    In your answer you must refer closely to the text and to at least two of: theme, characterisation, editing, aspects of mise-en scène, or any other appropriate feature.

17. Choose a film or TV drama* in which setting in time and/or place is significant.

    Explain why you think the setting is important for your appreciation of the text.

    In your answer you must refer closely to the text and to at least two of: setting, aspects of mise-en-scène, theme, soundtrack, or any other appropriate feature.

*"TV drama" may be a single play, series or serial.

[END OF QUESTION PAPER]

HIGHER SQP

[C115/SQP215]

NATIONAL
QUALIFICATIONS

Time: 1 hour 30 minutes

ENGLISH
HIGHER
Close Reading
Specimen Question Paper
(for examinations in and after 2003)

Answer all questions.

50 marks are allocated to this paper.

There are TWO passages and questions.

Read both passages carefully and then answer all the questions which follow. **Use your own words whenever possible and particularly when you are instructed to do so.**

You should read each passage to:

understand what the authors are saying about global warming and its effects (**Understanding—U**);

analyse their choices of language, imagery and structures to recognise how they convey their points of view and contribute to the impact of the passages (**Analysis—A**);

evaluate how effectively they have achieved their purposes (**Evaluation—E**).

A code letter (U, A, E) is used alongside each question to give some indication of the skills being assessed. The number of marks attached to each question will give some indication of the length of answer required.

SCOTTISH
QUALIFICATIONS
AUTHORITY

PASSAGE 1

This passage is from an article by journalist Angus Clark and appeared in The Times *newspaper in November 2000 after severe gales and extensive flooding in various parts of England.*

This is a tale of two towns: both modest, yet possessed of a certain civic pride; both nestled at the edge of the ocean, sharing almost exactly the same latitude. In Churchill, Manitoba, in
5 northern Canada, the winter is long, the snow is deep, the sea freezes far and wide as the thermometer falls to minus 50 degrees centigrade. There are only two months a year without snow. When the polar bears emerge from hibernation
10 they gnaw the dustbins in search of scraps. Churchill, in short, is not a place to grow wheat and roses, potatoes and apples. There are no green dairy farms on the tundra shores of Hudson's Bay. In Inverness, on the east coast of Scotland, the
15 winters are very much gentler and shorter. Cold, yes, but not cold enough for skidoos, treble-glazed windows or snowshoes to school. The nearby Black Isle has some of Scotland's richest arable farmland.

20 The enormous difference between the climates of these two towns is due to one thing: the Gulf Stream, which brings tropic-warmed sea from the Gulf of Mexico to the Atlantic coasts of northern Europe. Thanks to the Gulf Stream, on fine
25 summer days people can swim in the sea from the pale golden beaches of the Lofoten Islands in Norway—300 miles north of the Arctic Circle. In coastal gardens beside its warm waters, sub-tropical plants and exotic flowers flourish.

If there were no Gulf Stream, Britain would be as 30 cold as Manitoba. We would probably be able to walk to Germany across the frozen North Sea. Our farmers would be defeated by permafrost but caribou would thrive on the lichens beneath the snow. Dairy herds would not wind o'er the lea, nor 35 would honeysuckle twine about our cottage porches.

The Gulf Stream has not always flowed. As far as scientists can tell, it has stopped quite abruptly in the past—and in as little as a couple of years. Now 40 it seems that global warming is recreating the very same conditions which caused it to stall before, with the potential to plunge the whole of northern Europe into another Ice Age.

Which is a bit ironic as we slosh around in sodden, 45 rainswept towns and villages; as we discuss the extraordinary late autumn and give up hope for a white Christmas. Global warming was going to bring Mediterranean holiday weather to Brighton and vineyards to Argyll, wasn't it? Global 50 warming is the reason why spring-flowering iris and cistus are blooming crazily in November. So how could it turn England's green and rather tepid land into a frozen waste?

PASSAGE 2

The second passage, by James O. Jackson, appeared in Time *magazine also in November 2000.*

Deluges, droughts, fires, landslides, avalanches, gales, tornadoes; is it just our imagination, or is Europe's weather getting worse?

The short answer is yes, the weather is certainly
5 getting worse. The cause is air pollution that pours greenhouse gases such as carbon dioxide and methane into the atmosphere to produce global warming that can alter weather patterns. Whether the specific storms that scythed down trees in Paris
10 last Christmas, drowned the Po Valley last month and battered Britain last week can be attributed to the warming trend is a subject of serious—and contentious—scientific debate. But most climate experts agree that so-called extreme weather
15 events are becoming more frequent, and that the weather world-wide over the coming 100 years will change drastically. The scientists say that even if the world's governments and industries meet international goals on reducing greenhouse
20 gases—which they probably will not—it still won't be enough to prevent severe changes to the world's

weather. Their advice to governments, businesses and private citizens about this is grim: get used to it.

A landmark report released last week by a team of 25 27 European climatologists confirms that the trend in global warming may be irreversible, at least over most of the coming century. That, they say, means governments should start planning immediately to adapt to the new extremes of 30 weather that the citizens will face—with bans on building in potential flood plains in the north, for example, and water conservation measures in the south.

That represents a subtle but significant shift 35 in attitude to global warming and some environmentalist campaigners are dismayed at the suggestion that the world should adapt to the warming trend rather than try to halt or reverse it.

Next week at the Hague, representatives of 160 40 countries will gather to assess progress since the

1997 Kyoto Protocol. In that agreement, governments pledged that, by 2012, they would cut greenhouse emissions to 5·2% below 1992 levels. They are far from meeting that goal, and the Hague conference is likely to turn into a wrangle of finger-pointing over who is at fault. Campaigners for drastic cuts in emissions fear that talk of "adapting" rather than "mitigating" will ease political pressures on the big polluters such as the US and Japan.

All this because, says the Intergovernmental Panel on Climate Change, temperatures could rise by as much as 6 degrees centigrade in the 21st century, ten times as fast as temperatures have risen in the last 100 years. Who will want to live in such a world—especially in some of the regions likely to be hardest hit, which happen to include those already the poorest on the planet? Dry areas will get drier, wet areas will get wetter. Africa will suffer in ways that scientists cannot fully predict, but the Sahel will probably become even drier and more prone to drought and famine than it already is. For Europe, it will mean the influx of such pathogens as malaria, dengue fever and encephalitis as warmer weather encourages the northern movement of disease-carrying mosquitoes. Generally, warmer water can more easily harbour cholera and other waterborne diseases which will be more easily spread during frequent floods.

Some argue that the ultimate result of global warming will be a paradoxical but even more catastrophic development: global cooling. As the Arctic ice cap melts, a flow of fresh water into the North Atlantic could disrupt conveyer currents including the Gulf Stream, which is what keeps northern Europe warm. According to Steve Hall, oceanographer at Southampton Oceanography Centre, "One moment we could be basking in a Mediterranean climate and the next icebergs could be floating down the English Channel." It would take just one quarter of 1% more fresh water

flowing into the North Atlantic from melting Arctic glaciers to bring the northwards flow of the Gulf Stream to a halt.

And in August this year, a tremor of apprehension ran through the scientific community when the Russian ice-breaker *Yamal*, on a tourist cruise of the Arctic, muscled its way through unusually thin ice to the North Pole to find itself sailing serenely into an astonishingly clear blue sea. It was the first time the effects of global warming had been seen so far north.

Steve Hall's tongue may have been lodged firmly in cheek while making his prediction, and certainly few scientists believe the English iceberg scenario is likely even a century from now. Some, indeed, question the accuracy of most if not all of such apocalyptic predictions. "The science of climate change is enormously complicated," says Julian Morris, an environmental analyst at London's Institute of Economic Affairs. "The data are inconclusive, contradictory and confusing." Temperature measurements, for example, have been taken for only a relatively short period of time and may be skewed by such factors as urban expansion. The climatological history of the world is long, he says, and man's knowledge of it is short. "Attempting to make clear assessments of what is driving the climate over these much shorter time spans is fraught with difficulty." But the growing consensus is that momentous changes are coming.

Governments may stop finger-pointing and instead join hands; industries may slash short-term profit to permit long-term survival; populations may realise the cost and embrace huge changes in lifestyle. Only an optimist, though, and an uninformed optimist at that, could believe that humankind will succeed in making such radical changes in time to avert the bad weather ahead. So the best advice is to get out the umbrellas and hip boots and head for high ground. Storms are coming; the water is rising. We—and our descendants—will have to learn to live with it.

			Marks	Code

Questions on Passage 1

1. (a) By referring to lines 1–4, identify four features which make Churchill and Inverness similar. Use your own words as far as possible. — 2 U

(b) In lines 4–19, the writer contrasts the climate of these two towns. Show how the writer's use of language makes Churchill's climate seem more extreme than that of Inverness. — 4 A

2. (a) Explain briefly in your own words why the Gulf Stream, as described in lines 20–24, affects the climate of northern Europe. — 1 U

(b) Show how the writer uses contrast in lines 24–37 to illustrate the impact of the Gulf Stream. You should refer to specific words and phrases in your answer. — 4 A

3. Consider lines 38–54.

(a) Explain the meaning of "stall" as it is used in line 42. — 1 U

(b) (i) What is "ironic" (line 45) about the possible effect of global warming on northern Europe? — 2 U

(ii) Show how the writer, in lines 45–54, emphasises this irony. In your answer, you should refer to such features as sentence structure, tone, word choice. — 4 A

(18)

Questions on Passage 2

4. (a) Explain how any one language feature in lines 1–3 helps to make dramatic the opening of the article. — 2 A

(b) Explain, using your own words as far as possible, why the weather is "getting worse". You should refer to lines 4–8 in your answer. — 2 U

(c) Show how the writer uses imagery in lines 8–13 to emphasise the impact of the storms which affected Europe. You should refer to two examples in your answer. — 4 A

(d) Show how the writer helps to clarify his argument in lines 17–24 by using:

(i) dashes;

(ii) a colon. — 2 A

5. Consider lines 25–39.

What is the "shift in attitude" (lines 35–36)? — 2 U

6. By referring to lines 40–51, explain briefly in your own words two problems which may emerge at the Hague conference. — 2 U

7. (a) In lines 52–86, the writer describes the possible effects of global warming. Using your own words as far as possible, outline briefly the main effects on Africa, on Europe, and on the North Atlantic. — 5 U

(b) In the context of global warming, how effective do you find the writer's anecdote about the *Yamal* (lines 87–94)? Justify your answer. — 2 E

8. By referring to lines 95–113, give two reasons why the situation might not be as bleak as is being suggested by many of the scientists. Use your own words as far as possible. — 2 U

9. To what extent would you agree that the final paragraph (lines 114–125) is an effective conclusion to the article? Justify your answer by referring to such features as ideas, punctuation, tone, imagery, point of view. — 3 E

(26)

Question on both Passages

10. Which of the two writers appears to treat the topic of global warming more effectively? Justify your choice by referring to such features as ideas, tone, use of examples, style. You should refer to both passages in your answer. — 6 E

[END OF SPECIMEN QUESTION PAPER]

Total (50)

[C115/SQP215]

NATIONAL
QUALIFICATIONS

Time: 1 hour 30 minutes

ENGLISH
HIGHER
Critical Essay
Specimen Question Paper
(for examinations in and after 2003)

Answer **two** questions.

Each question must be taken from a different section.

Each question in worth 25 marks.

SCOTTISH
QUALIFICATIONS
AUTHORITY

©

Answer TWO questions from this paper.

Each question must be chosen from a different Section (A–E). You are not allowed to choose two questions from the same Section.

In all Sections you may use Scottish texts.

Write the number of each question in the margin of your answer booklet and begin each essay on a fresh page. You should spend about 45 minutes on each essay.

The following will be assessed:

* the relevance of your essays to the questions you have chosen

* the quality of your writing

* the technical accuracy of your writing.

Each answer is worth up to 25 marks. The total for this paper is 50 marks.

SECTION A—DRAMA

1. Choose a play in which there is a scene dominated by confusion, complications or uncertainties.

    Explain the cause(s) of the confusion, complications or uncertainties, and go on to discuss the importance of the scene to your appreciation of the play as a whole.

    In your answer you must refer closely to the text and to at least two of: structure, dialogue, conflict, theme, or any other appropriate feature.

2. Choose a play in which a character keeps something hidden or pretends to be something she or he is not.

    Explain the reason(s) for the character's behaviour and discuss how it affects your attitude to the character.

    In your answer you must refer closely to the text and to at least two of: characterisation, dramatic irony, theme, soliloquy, or any other appropriate feature.

3. Choose a play whose main theme is made clear early in the action.

    Show how the dramatist introduces the theme and discuss how successfully he or she goes on to develop it.

    In your answer you must refer closely to the text and to at least two of: theme, key scene(s), characterisation, language, or any other appropriate feature.

4. Choose a play in which one scene or moment determines the fate of a main character.

    Explain fully why you think this is the key moment in the character's fortunes.

    In your answer you must refer closely to the text and to at least two of: key scene, characterisation, climax, dialogue, or any other appropriate feature.

SECTION B—PROSE

5. Choose a **novel** which is influenced by the presence of a powerful or overbearing character.

    Show how the novelist creates this impression of the character and discuss to what extent you felt you could sympathise with him or her.

    In your answer you must refer closely to the text and to at least two of: characterisation, narrative technique, language, theme, or any other appropriate feature.

6. Choose a **novel** or **short story** in which a family disagreement plays an important part.

    Explain the circumstances of the disagreement and show how the writer uses it to develop theme and/or character.

    In your answer you must refer closely to the text and to at least two of: theme, setting, plot, characterisation, or any other appropriate feature.

7. Choose a **novel** or **short story** with a dramatic or shocking ending.

    Show how the writer creates the effect and discuss to what extent it added to your appreciation of the text as a whole.

    In your answer you must refer closely to the text and to at least two of: structure, climax, theme, characterisation, or any other appropriate feature.

8. Choose a **novel** in which the novelist makes effective use of symbolism.

    Show how the writer made use of this technique to enhance your appreciation of the text as a whole.

    In your answer you must refer closely to the text and to at least two of: symbolism, theme, imagery, structure, or any other appropriate feature.

9. Choose a **non-fiction text** which introduced you to a new culture.

    Explain how well the writer achieved that introduction.

    In your answer you must refer closely to the text and to at least two of: narrative voice, ideas, setting, structure, use of anecdote or any other appropriate feature.

10. Choose a **non-fiction text** which made you think about an environmental issue.

    Explain briefly what the issue is and at greater length show how the writer's treatment of the issue conveyed her or his point of view.

    In your answer you must refer closely to the text and to at least two of: ideas, point of view, use of evidence, organisation, use of examples or any other appropriate feature.

11. Choose a **non-fiction text** which presented the life story of a particular person.

    Evaluate the techniques the author used to make the biography enjoyable.

    In your answer you must refer closely to the text and to at least two of: narrative voice, language, anecdote, structure, or any other appropriate feature.

SECTION C—POETRY

12. Choose a poem which is light-hearted or playful or not entirely serious.

    Show how the poet makes you aware of the tone, and discuss how effective the use of this tone is in dealing with the subject matter of the poem.

    In your answer you must refer closely to the text and to at least two of: tone, imagery, theme, sound, or any other appropriate feature.

13. Choose two poems on the subject of war or hostility.

    Compare the way the two poems treat the subject, and explain to what extent you find one more effective than the other.

    In your answer you must refer closely to the text and to at least two of: theme, structure, imagery, rhythm and rhyme, or any other appropriate feature.

14. Choose a poem which depicts one of the following: the sea, the night, the countryside, sleep, a dream, travel.

    Show how the poet brings the subject to life for you.

    In your answer you must refer closely to the text and to at least two of: imagery, atmosphere, sound, theme, or any other appropriate feature.

15. Choose a poem which explores loneliness or isolation.

    Show how the poet explores the theme, and discuss to what extent your appreciation of the theme was deepened by the poet's treatment.

    In your answer you must refer closely to the text and to at least two of: theme, mood, imagery, contrast, or any other appropriate feature.

SECTION D—MASS MEDIA

16. Choose a film which has a particularly effective or arresting opening.

    Referring in detail to the opening, discuss to what extent it provides a successful introduction to the text as a whole.

    In your answer you must refer closely to the text and to at least two of: aspects of mise-en-scène, structure, editing, soundtrack, or any other appropriate feature.

17. Choose from a film or TV drama* a scene in which the conflict between two characters is at its most intense.

    Outline briefly the reasons for the conflict and then by examining the scene in detail, show how it gave you a deeper appreciation of the text as a whole.

    In your answer you must refer closely to the text and to at least two of: key scene, characterisation, dialogue, aspects of mise-en-scène, or any other appropriate feature.

18. Choose a TV drama* in which the character struggles with her or his conscience.

    Outline briefly the reasons for the character's dilemma and go on to discuss how successfully the programme-makers engage your sympathy for her or him.

    In your answer you must refer closely to the text and to at least two of: theme, characterisation, editing, aspects of mise-en scène, or any other appropriate feature.

19. Choose a film or TV drama* in which setting in time and/or place is significant.

    Explain why you think the setting is important for your appreciation of the text.

    In your answer you must refer closely to the text and to at least two of: setting, aspects of mise-en-scène, theme, soundtrack, or any other appropriate feature.

*"TV drama" may be a single play, series or serial.

SECTION E—LANGUAGE

20. Choose an aspect of language which you have investigated within a specific interest group in society.

    Identify the kind of group or groups you investigated, making clear what it was they had in common. Show to what extent the specialist language connected with the interest of the group(s) increased the effectiveness of communication within the group(s).

    You must refer to specific examples, and to at least two language concepts such as jargon, register, technical terminology, abbreviations or any other appropriate concept.

21. Choose an aspect of communication technology, such as TV, e-mail, mobile phone, which has brought about developments in our language in the last decade.

    Explain the nature of the developments you have investigated and evaluate what impact they had on the effectiveness of communication.

    You must refer to specific examples and to at least two language concepts such as jargon, register, orthography or any other appropriate concept.

22. Choose an aspect of spoken language which you have investigated within a particular age group.

    Briefly describe the parameters of your investigation. Show how far the language characteristics of the group you investigated differed from the general population and go on to evaluate the advantages and disadvantages of these differences.

    You must refer to specific examples and to at least two language concepts such as register, dialect, accent, vocabulary or any other appropriate concept.

23. Choose an area of communication in which emotive language is commonly used to influence the reader, viewer or listener.

    Outline the purposes of the communication(s) you have chosen. Go on to analyse the methods used and evaluate the effectiveness of the communication in achieving its purpose.

    You must refer to specific examples and to at least two language concepts such as word choice, tone, presentation, structure, or any other appropriate concept.

[END OF SPECIMEN QUESTION PAPER]

[BLANK PAGE]

2003 HIGHER

X115/301

NATIONAL
QUALIFICATIONS
2003

FRIDAY, 16 MAY
9.00 AM – 10.30 AM

ENGLISH
HIGHER
Close Reading

Answer all questions.

50 marks are allocated to this paper.

There are TWO passages and questions.

Read the passages carefully and then answer all the questions which follow. **Use your own words whenever possible and particularly when you are instructed to do so.**

You should read the passages to:

understand what the writers are saying about refugees, asylum seekers, and immigration in general (**Understanding—U**);

analyse their choices of language, imagery and structures to recognise how they convey their points of view and contribute to the impact of the passages (**Analysis—A**);

evaluate how effectively they have achieved their purposes (**Evaluation—E**).

A code letter (U, A, E) is used alongside each question to give some indication of the skills being assessed. The number of marks attached to each question will give some indication of the length of answer required.

SCOTTISH
QUALIFICATIONS
AUTHORITY

PASSAGE 1

The first passage is an article in The Herald *newspaper in June 2002. In it, journalist and broadcaster Ruth Wishart offers some thoughts on attitudes to immigration to Scotland.*

CAN BRITAIN AFFORD TO KEEP TALENTED IMMIGRANTS OUT?

If you hail from Glasgow you will have friends or relatives whose roots lie in the Irish Republic. You will have Jewish friends or colleagues whose grandparents, a good number of them Polish or
5 Russian, may have fled persecution in Europe. You will eat in premises run by Italian or French proprietors. It is a diverse cultural heritage enriched now by a large and vibrant Asian population and a smaller but significant Chinese
10 one.

It was not always thus.

The city census of 1831 found 47 Jewish citizens, a community which grew and prospered as it became an integral part of Glasgow's merchant
15 growth. The first Asian immigrants were no more than a few young men, largely from poor and rural backgrounds, whose early employment as door-to-door salesmen gave no hint of the entrepreneurial flair their heirs and successors
20 would bring to so many trade sectors in the city.

The early Italians found the route to Glaswegian hearts through their stomachs as they set up chains of chip shops and ice-cream parlours; the
25 Chinese, too, helped the local palate become rather more discerning when they began to arrive in numbers half a century ago.

All of these immigrant populations have two things in common: they were economic migrants and their effect on their adopted homeland has
30 been, almost without exception, a beneficial one. That is a lesson from history some of our more hysteria-prone politicians would do well to ponder as they devise ever more unfriendly welcomes for those who would come here today to live and work.

35 This week the Home Secretary was assuring his French counterpart that Britain would clamp down even more severely on those working here illegally. At the same time plans are advanced for "accommodation centres", which will have the
40 immediate effect of preventing natural integration, while children of immigrants are to be denied the harmonising effect of inter-racial schooling. Meanwhile, ever more sophisticated technology is to be employed to stem the numbers
45 of young men who risk their lives clinging to the underside of trains and lorries, or are paying obscene sums of money to the 21st century's own version of slave traders—those traffickers in human misery who make their fortunes on the
50 back of others' desperation.

Yet at the heart of this ever more draconian approach to immigration policy lie a number of misconceptions. The UK is not a group of nations swamped by a tidal wave of immigration.
55 Relatively speaking, Europe contends with a trickle of refugees compared with countries who border areas of famine, desperate poverty, or violent political upheaval. The countries of origin of the highest numbers coming here change from
60 year to year, depending on the hotspots of global conflict. A significant proportion of refugees want nothing more than to be able to return to that homeland when conditions allow.

But, whether they are transient or would-be
65 settlers, they face an uphill battle trying to find legal employment. People with real skills and talents to offer us find themselves in the black economy, or unemployed, because of a sluggish system of processing applications, allied to
70 regulations which preclude the legal marketplace.

Surely the most sensible way to "crack down" on illegal workers is to permit legal alternatives. Not just because of woolly liberalism—though that's a perfectly decent instinct—but because of
75 enlightened self-interest. Recently, I was reading an analysis of what was happening to the economy in the Highlands and Islands. The writer welcomes the fact that the population of that area has gone up 20% in one generation. But he goes
80 on to say that "labour shortages of every kind are becoming the biggest single constraint in the way of additional economic expansion." He adds: "In principle the solution to this problem is readily available in the shape of the so-called asylum
85 seekers or economic migrants that our country, like most countries, seems determined to turn away."

While, for the most part, immigrants to the Highlands and Islands have recently come from England, the future lies in casting the net much
90 wider. That would be, after all, yet another Scottish solution to a Scottish problem, given that this nation regularly suffers from population loss, exporting tranches of economic migrants all over the world every year. It's been something of a
95 national hobby, which is why there is almost no corner of the globe where you won't stumble over a Caledonian society enthusiastically peopled by folks who will do anything for the old country bar live in it.
100

Yet Ireland has managed to attract its young entrepreneurs back to help drive a burgeoning economy. We must try to do likewise. We need

immigrants. We cannot grow the necessary skills
105 fast enough to fill the gap sites. We need people
with energy and commitment and motivation,
three characteristics commonly found among those
whose circumstances prompt them to make huge
sacrifices to find a new life.

110 Round about now, families all over Scotland will be
waving their newly graduated offspring off on the
increasingly popular gap year between university
and real life. Most of them will have a ball, finding

enough work to keep the adventure on the road as
they travel. Some of them won't come back at all, 115
having found a good job or a soulmate elsewhere.
Provided they stay on the right side of the law, very
few of them will be harassed by customs officials,
locked up in detention centres while their papers
are checked, or deported for overstaying their 120
welcome. If you're one of us and sort of solvent,
come into the parlour, there's a welcome there for
you.

PASSAGE 2

The second passage is adapted from an essay in The Guardian *newspaper, also in June 2002. In it, Anne Karpf
explores past and present press coverage of immigration issues and tells the story of one family from Kosovo who
sought asylum in Britain.*

WE HAVE BEEN HERE BEFORE

There's a melancholy little game that staff at the
Refugee Council sometimes play. They show
visitors press cuttings about refugees and asylum
seekers from the 1900s, 1930s and today, and ask
5 them to guess when they were published. Most
people get it wrong. They assume that Jewish
refugees were welcomed, at least in the 1930s, with
a tolerance that has traditionally been seen as a
beacon of Britishness. They're shocked to discover
10 that rabid intolerance has a strong British pedigree.

And the press has persisted in peddling incorrect
figures about immigration. One newspaper's
assertion in 1938 that there were more Jews in
Britain than Germany ever had, was plain wrong.
15 Similarly, the tabloids' current depiction of Britain
as an international magnet for asylum seekers is
totally misleading. Most of the world's refugees do
what they've always done: they move from one poor
country to another, usually a neighbouring one.
20 Only a tiny percentage make it to the richer
countries: 5% to Europe, and less than 1% to
Britain. A regular peruser of the press today,
however, with its loose talk of "swamping" and
"floods", would be stunned to learn that, of 15 EU
25 countries, Britain stands at number 10 in the
number of asylum seekers per head of population.

The asylum seeker has become a composite, almost
mythical figure. Despite the allegedly vast
numbers of them now in the country, most British
30 people have never actually met one, making it all
the easier to dehumanise them.

But what does real asylum-seeking feel like?
Thirty-one-year-old Arberore arrived with her
husband, Petrit, and their two-year-old son Norik
35 from Pristina, Kosovo, in 1995 as illegal asylum
seekers. Petrit, a travel agent, had been questioned
and threatened on many occasions by Serb police,
while Arberore, an architecture student, could no
longer attend the university because it was closed to
40 Albanians. "We felt that we were in danger," she
says, "but it was a very difficult decision to leave
because we were a very close-knit community."

They arrived in Britain on false papers. "It was

very scary—it was the first time in my life that I lied
like that. I felt terrible. Petrit's hand was shaking 45
when he handed over the papers." Upon arrival,
they went straight to the Home Office, to tell them
that they'd entered with false papers. "They didn't
threaten to deport us, because we had a child," says
Arberore, "but we were scared. We spent the day 50
waiting in the Home Office. I felt so happy that I
wasn't any longer in Kosovo to be frightened, but I
felt like a beggar that day. We had to be
fingerprinted. I thought I was going to prison." It
took them two years to get legal asylum. 55

I showed Arberore, now a student at Middlesex
University, some press cuttings on asylum seekers.
She was particularly shocked by one headline
A DOOR WE CAN'T CLOSE. She said, "It
makes me feel like vermin." And of another GET 60
THEM OUT, she demanded, "Who wrote that? It
makes me feel as if I'm no one. I can give something
to this country. But I want to say to these reporters:
we're all human beings and who knows when
British people might need someone's help? We left 65
everything there: we had a job, a huge house and a
garden; we had a nice life. But the most important
thing was our freedom."

Rabbi Hugo Gryn once said: "How you are with
someone to whom you owe nothing is a grave test." 70
At the moment, Britain is failing that test,
especially in its press coverage. The reporting of
prewar Jewish asylum seekers is shocking because
we know how that story ended. But instead of using
hindsight to idealise, we can use it to illuminate. 75
Let us learn this much at least: hostile reporting of
asylum seekers dispossesses them yet again.
Refugees seek asylum from hate or destitution, and
then run into it once more. As the daughter of
postwar Polish Jewish asylum seekers, I'm 80
stupefied by how the collective memory can be so
short, bigotry so blatant, and how, with all the
recent interest in the Holocaust, basic connections
can fail to be made. Are we doomed always to
stigmatise the stranger? Must compassion only 85
ever be extended after the event?

	Marks	Code
Questions on Passage 1		

1. Look at the first paragraph (lines 1–10).

   (a) By referring closely to these lines, show how you are helped to understand the meaning of the expression "diverse cultural heritage" (line 7). — 2 — U

   (b) Referring to **one** example of effective word choice in this paragraph, show how the writer makes clear her positive attitude to the people she is describing. — 2 — A

2. Comment on the impact of line 11 in helping the writer to develop her line of thought. — 2 — A

3. From lines 12–26, identify briefly and in your own words as far as possible:

   (a) **two** similarities between Jewish and Asian immigrants to Glasgow; — 2 — U

   (b) **one** similarity between Italian and Chinese immigrants to Glasgow. — 1 — U

4. Read lines 27–50.

   (a) Explain in your own words the "two things" which, according to the writer, "all of these immigrant populations . . . have in common" (lines 27–28). — 2 — U

   (b) Show how the writer's word choice in the sentence "That is . . . and work" (lines 31–34) makes clear her attitude to certain politicians. Refer to **two** examples in your answer. — 2 — A

   (c) How does the writer's language make clear her disapproval of any **one** of the proposed measures referred to in lines 35–50? — 2 — A

5. (a) Referring to specific words or phrases, show how the sentence "Yet . . . misconceptions" (lines 51–53) performs a linking function in the writer's line of thought. — 2 — U

   (b) Discuss how effective you find the writer's use of imagery in lines 51–70 in making her point clear. You may refer in your answer to one or more examples. — 2 — E

6. Read carefully lines 71–100.

Using your own words as far as possible, outline **three** important points which are made in these paragraphs to develop the argument about immigration. — 3 — U

7. Show how the writer uses sentence structure **or** tone to demonstrate her strength of feeling in lines 101–109. — 2 — A

8. The writer concludes with a reference to Scottish students and the "gap year". How effective do you find this illustration as a conclusion to the passage as a whole? — 2 — E

(26)

Questions on Passage 2		

9. Look at the opening paragraph (lines 1–10).

   (a) What is the purpose of the "little game that staff at the Refugee Council sometimes play"? — 1 — U

   (b) Select **one** example of imagery from these lines and explain how the writer uses it to make her point clear. — 2 — A

10. Look at lines 11–26.

   (a) Using your own words as far as possible, explain briefly how the writer illustrates the idea that "the press has persisted in peddling incorrect figures about immigration" (lines 11–12). — 2 — U

   (b) Show how the writer's language in lines 11–26 demonstrates her disapproval of the press. — 2 — A

11. " . . . a composite, almost mythical figure" (lines 27–28).

   (a) Explain this expression in your own words. — 2 — U

   (b) Explain why, according to lines 27–31, the asylum seeker is now regarded in this way. — 1 — U

12. (a) In lines 32–55, the writer tells the story of a "real asylum-seeking" family.

Discuss how successful you think the writer has been in convincing you that this is a "real" story. In your answer you should refer closely to specific features of the writing. — 4 — A/E

   (b) By referring to tone **or** to sentence structure in lines 56–68, show how you are made aware of how strongly Arberore feels about the press cuttings. — 2 — A

13. Show how the final paragraph (lines 69–86) brings the passage to an emotional conclusion. — 3 — A

(19)

Question on both Passages		

14. Which passage has given you a clearer understanding of key issues concerning immigration and asylum-seeking? You should refer in your answer to the main ideas of both passages. — 5 — U/E

[END OF QUESTION PAPER]   **Total (50)**

X115/302

NATIONAL
QUALIFICATIONS
2003

FRIDAY, 16 MAY
10.50 AM – 12.20 PM

ENGLISH
HIGHER
Critical Essay

Answer **two** questions.

Each question must be taken from a different section.

Each question is worth 25 marks.

SCOTTISH
QUALIFICATIONS
AUTHORITY

©

Answer TWO questions from this paper.

Each question must be chosen from a different Section (A–E). You are not allowed to choose two questions from the same Section.

In all Sections you may use Scottish texts.

Write the number of each question chosen in the margin of your answer booklet and begin each essay on a fresh page. You should spend about 45 minutes on each essay.

The following will be assessed:

*   **the relevance of your essays to the questions you have chosen**

*   **the quality of your answers**

*   **the technical accuracy of your writing.**

Each answer is worth up to 25 marks. The total for this paper is 50 marks.

SECTION A—DRAMA

1. Choose a play in which a character feels increasingly isolated from the community in which he or she lives.

    Show how the dramatist makes you aware of the character's increasing isolation and discuss how it affects your attitude to the character.

    In your answer you must refer closely to the text and to at least **two** of: characterisation, soliloquy, key scene(s), setting, or any other appropriate feature.

2. Choose a play in which the dramatist explores conflict between opposing values or ideas.

    Show how the dramatist makes you aware of the conflict and discuss the extent to which you find the resolution of the conflict satisfying.

    In your answer you must refer closely to the text and to at least **two** of: structure, theme, key scene(s), characterisation, or any other appropriate feature.

3. Choose a play in which there is a scene which provides a clear turning point in the drama.

    Explain why it is a turning point and go on to discuss the importance of the scene to your appreciation of the play as a whole.

    In your answer you must refer closely to the text and to at least **two** of: structure, theme, dialogue, conflict, or any other appropriate feature.

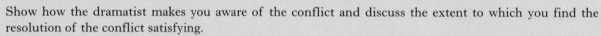

4. Choose a play in which there is a breakdown in family relationship(s).

    Explain the reason(s) for the breakdown and discuss the extent to which it is important to the play as a whole.

    In your answer you must refer closely to the text and to at least **two** of: theme, dialogue, characterisation, conflict, or any other appropriate feature.

SECTION B—PROSE

5. Choose a **novel** which caused you to reconsider your views on an important human issue.

   Explain what the issue is and go on to discuss how the writer made you reconsider your views.

   In your answer you must refer closely to the text and to at least **two** of: theme, narrative stance, characterisation, climax, or any other appropriate feature.

6. Choose a **novel** or **short story** in which a conflict between two of the main characters is central to the story.

   Explain how the conflict arises and go on to discuss in detail how the writer uses it to explore an important theme.

   In your answer you must refer closely to the text and to at least **two** of: characterisation, key incident(s), structure, setting, or any other appropriate feature.

7. Choose a **novel** which you enjoyed because of the effectiveness of its ending.

   Explain how the ending satisfies you and adds to your appreciation of the novel.

   In your answer you must refer closely to the text and to at least **two** of: climax, theme, characterisation, plot, or any other appropriate feature.

8. Choose a **novel** or **short story** in which a technique (such as symbolism) is used by the author and is, in your view, vital to the success of the text.

   Explain how the writer employs this technique and why, in your opinion, it is so important to your appreciation of the text.

   In your answer you must refer closely to the text and to its theme as well as to the writer's use of your chosen technique.

9. Choose a **non-fiction text** which influenced your views about a scientific or a health-related issue.

   Outline the nature of the issue and explain how the writer's presentation influenced your views.

   In your answer you must refer closely to the text and to at least **two** of: ideas, use of evidence, structure, stance, or any other appropriate feature.

10. Choose a **non-fiction text** which tells the life story of someone who captured your interest.

    Give a brief account of what was notable about the person's achievements. Go on to discuss how the writer's presentation confirmed or changed your opinion of the individual's life.

    In your answer you must refer closely to the text and to at least **two** of: selection of information, language, narrative voice, anecdote, or any other appropriate feature.

11. Choose a **non-fiction text** which is set in a society which is different from your own.

    Explain what is significantly different and discuss how effectively the writer made you aware of this.

    In your answer you must refer closely to the text and to at least **two** of: ideas, setting in time or place, narrative voice, language, or any other appropriate feature.

[Turn over

SECTION C—POETRY

12. Choose two nature poems.

    Compare each poem's treatment of the subject, and discuss which you find more successful.

    In your answer you must refer closely to the text and to at least **two** of: atmosphere, structure, theme, imagery, or any other appropriate feature.

13. Choose a poem in which you feel there is a significant moment which reveals the central idea of the poem.

    Show how the poet achieves this in an effective way.

    In your answer you must refer closely to the text and to at least **two** of: structure, mood, imagery, ideas, or any other appropriate feature.

14. Choose a poem in which the poet has created a perfect blend of form and content.

    Show how the poet achieves this and discuss how it adds to your appreciation of the poem.

    In your answer you must refer closely to the text and to at least **two** of: form, theme, word choice, rhythm, or any other appropriate feature.

15. Choose a poem which explores **either** the significance of the past **or** the importance of family relationships.

    Show how the poet treats the subject, and explain to what extent you find the treatment convincing.

    In your answer you must refer closely to the text and to at least **two** of: theme, imagery, rhyme, tone, or any other appropriate feature.

SECTION D—MASS MEDIA

16. Choose a film in which one of the characters is corrupted by the society which surrounds him/her.

    Briefly describe how the corruption takes hold, and go on to show how the film maker involves you in the fate of the character.

    In your answer you must refer closely to the text and to at least **two** of: characterisation, mise-en-scène, theme, editing, or any other appropriate feature.

17. Choose a film in which there is a sequence creating a high degree of tension.

    Show what techniques are employed to create and sustain the tension in this sequence and how, in the context of the whole film, it adds to your viewing experience.

    In your answer you must refer closely to the text and to at least **two** of: editing, use of camera, soundtrack, mise-en-scène, or any other appropriate feature.

18. Choose a film or *TV drama which deals with a topical issue in a memorable way.

    Explain briefly what the issue is, and go on to discuss how your interest and emotions were engaged by the treatment of the issue in the film or *TV drama.

    In your answer you must refer closely to the text and to at least **two** of: theme, characterisation, mise-en-scène, structure, or any other appropriate feature.

19. Choose a film or *TV drama which makes a major part of its impact through the detailed recreation of a period setting.

    Discuss to what extent the setting contributed to your understanding of the concerns of the society depicted in the film or *TV drama.

    In your answer you must refer closely to the text and to at least **two** of: mise-en-scène, theme, music, editing, or any other appropriate feature.

*"TV drama" includes a single play, a series or a serial.

SECTION E—LANGUAGE

20. Consider an aspect of language which shows development over time.

    Describe the changes which you have identified, and evaluate the gains and losses to the language.

    You must refer to specific examples, and to at least **two** of the following: vocabulary, register, grammar, idiom, or any other appropriate concept.

21. Consider some aspects of language which you have identified within a particular vocational group.

    Identify some of the characteristics of the language within such a group and evaluate the advantages and disadvantages for the group and the wider public.

    You must refer to specific examples and to at least **two** of the following: jargon, register, technical terminology, abbreviations, or any other appropriate concept.

22. Consider the language associated with any one form of electronic communication.

    Show how this language has developed and discuss to what extent it has made communication more effective.

    You must refer to specific examples and to at least **two** of the following: register, technical terminology, word choice, tone, or any other appropriate concept.

23. Consider your personal use of language in different contexts.

    Describe your use of language in at least two contexts, and discuss to what extent your communication varies in effectiveness from context to context.

    You must refer to specific examples and to at least **two** of the following: register, dialect, accent, vocabulary, or any other appropriate concept.

[END OF QUESTION PAPER]